ALTERNATIVE ENERGY

OCEAN ENERGY

by Laura K. Murray

Content Consultant
Andrea E. Copping, PhD
Senior Scientist, Marine Renewable Energy
Pacific Northwest National Laboratory

Core Library

An Imprint of Abdo Publishing
abdopublishing.com

abdopublishing.com

Published by Abdo Publishing, a division of ABDO, PO Box 398166, Minneapolis, Minnesota 55439. Copyright © 2017 by Abdo Consulting Group, Inc. International copyrights reserved in all countries. No part of this book may be reproduced in any form without written permission from the publisher. Core Library™ is a trademark and logo of Abdo Publishing.

Printed in the United States of America, North Mankato, Minnesota
082016
012017

 THIS BOOK CONTAINS RECYCLED MATERIALS

Cover Photo: Fred Tanneau/AFP/Getty Images
Interior Photos: Fred Tanneau/AFP/Getty Images, 1; US Navy, 4; Bob Bush Photo/iStockphoto, 6, 45; Mark Garlic/Science Source, 9; Maurice Tsai/Bloomberg/Getty Images, 12; Martin Bond/ Science Source, 14, 21, 24, 37, 43; Ipsumpix/Corbis/Getty Images, 17; Keystone-France/ Gamma-Rapho/Getty Images, 19; Red Line Editorial, 28; Van D. Bucher/Science Source, 30; Henning Bagger/AFP/Getty Images, 32; John F. Williams/US Navy, 34; Paul Mcerlane/ Bloomberg/Getty Images, 39

Editor: Arnold Ringstad
Series Designer: Nikki Farinella

Publisher's Cataloging-in-Publication Data

Names: Murray, Laura K., author.
Title: Ocean energy / by Laura K. Murray.
Description: Minneapolis, MN : Abdo Publishing, 2017. | Series: Alternative
    energy | Includes bibliographical references and index.
Identifiers: LCCN 2016945414 | ISBN 9781680784589 (lib. bdg.) |
    ISBN 9781680798432 (ebook)
Subjects: LCSH: Ocean energy resources--Juvenile literature. | Renewable energy
    sources--Juvenile literature.
 Classification: DDC 621.31--dc23
LC record available at http://lccn.loc.gov/2016945414

CONTENTS

MAKING WAVES

It is a warm June day in 2015. Off the coast of Oahu, Hawaii, puffy clouds move over the Wave Energy Test Site. The site is near Kaneohe Bay. A team of scientists, engineers, divers, and others are hard at work. Some are aboard boats, and others are in the water. They are setting up a 45-short-ton (40.8-metric-ton) test device. It has two

Many types of wave energy devices are tested near Hawaii's Kaneohe Bay.

The churning waters of the world's oceans can be harnessed to generate electricity.

bright yellow posts. This device will make electricity from the ocean's waves.

The device is called Azura. The electricity it generates will run along undersea cables to reach homes. A company called Northwest Energy Innovations developed Azura. Over the next year, scientists plan to gather information from the device. The US Navy and the US Department of Energy are also working on the project. They hope it will help them

Earth's Ocean

Earth's large body of water is known as the global ocean. That ocean is split into five areas. People today know them as the Atlantic, Pacific, Indian, Arctic, and Southern oceans. All these areas have much left to explore. Scientists believe hundreds of thousands of ocean species have not yet been discovered. Twelve people have walked on the moon, but as of 2016, only three humans had traveled to the deepest part of the ocean. This place is known as Challenger Deep. It is located in the western Pacific Ocean. It is approximately 36,070 feet (10,994 m) deep.

develop more technology to capture the power of ocean waves.

Soon Azura is in place. Its two posts bob upright in the water. Within just one month, scientists report exciting news. Azura has become the first wave energy device in the United States to supply electricity to a power grid.

Ocean Energy

The ocean covers approximately 71 percent of Earth's surface. It holds 97 percent of Earth's water. It also holds incredible power. The ocean's waves, currents, temperature, and salinity are all sources of energy. Ocean energy technology turns these sources of energy into electricity. Scientists and engineers are closely studying how ocean energy might help power our future. This type of energy is also called marine energy.

Ocean energy is renewable. This means it will never run out. Other renewable energy sources include sunlight, wind, and river water. They are seen

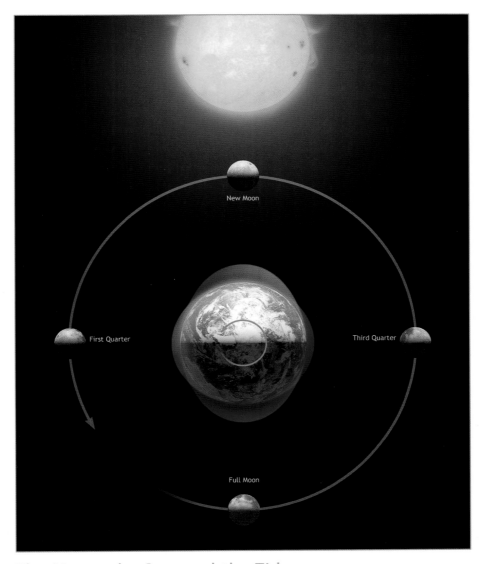

New Moon

First Quarter

Third Quarter

Full Moon

The Moon, the Sun, and the Tides

The gravitational pull of the moon and the sun are responsible for creating Earth's tides. Though the sun is larger than the moon, its great distance from Earth means that it exerts only half the moon's tidal influence. This diagram shows how the positions of the moon and sun affect the height of tides. When they are on the same side of Earth, the highest tides are created. Why might this be?

Water Planet

The ocean makes life on Earth possible. It plays a key role in the planet's weather, temperature, and climate. Even the ocean's very small creatures are important. Plankton are organisms that drift or float in the water. They are at the base of the ocean food web. Plants in the ocean make about half of the oxygen humans and land animals need. The ocean is important to humans in other ways too. It is used for food, transportation, waste disposal, and global trade.

as clean alternatives to fossil fuels, such as coal. When fossil fuels are burned to release energy, they produce large amounts of harmful greenhouse gases.

Ocean energy technology is in the early stages of development. It is growing slowly. But that could change in the coming years. People are becoming more interested in renewable energy sources. The amount of renewable energy made around the world could triple by the year 2035. Experts in the field believe ocean energy is one of the most exciting new types of renewable energy.

Harvesting Ocean Power

People harvest ocean energy in several ways. Two of these technologies are tidal and wave power. They use the motion of water to generate electricity. A third is ocean thermal energy conversion (OTEC). OTEC generates energy from temperature differences in the water.

Harvesting ocean power comes with challenges. One challenge is its high cost. Another challenge is the ocean environment itself. Its waves, harsh weather, deep waters, and salt make it a difficult place to work. These conditions make it hard to install and use the devices that generate electricity. Ocean energy technology still needs a lot of development. Engineers need to figure out how to move the energy to places on land where it is needed. Some people also worry about negative effects on the ocean and its animals.

But ocean energy has clear benefits too. It creates little to no pollution. As a renewable source, it will

Engineers in the island nation of Taiwan have developed OTEC research stations.

not run out. It might become cheaper than other renewable sources. Ocean energy could even be combined with wind energy. In addition, the ocean's waves and tides are reliable. Wind energy does not work on a calm day, but the ocean's water is constantly moving. OTEC has another bonus: in some cases it creates desalinated water. This is water with its salt removed. Desalinating water makes it safe for drinking or farming.

A Future of Energy

Today many scientists and engineers are studying ocean energy. They are gathering data using Azura and other test devices. They are developing new technologies. They want to find ways to best use the ocean's vast energy resources.

FURTHER EVIDENCE

Chapter One has information about Earth's ocean. What was one of the main points of this chapter? What key evidence supports this point? Read the article at the website below. Does information on the website support the main point of this chapter? Does it present new evidence?

Ocean Facts

mycorelibrary.com/ocean-energy

CHAPTER TWO

THE HISTORY OF OCEAN POWER

Humans have experimented with ocean power for many centuries. Europeans used tide mills as early as 787 CE. Tide mills used the rise and fall of the tides to turn a waterwheel. The wheel created mechanical power. This power was used for milling grain.

The scientific study of the oceans developed further in the 1600s. In 1609 German astronomer

Traditional tide mills have been in use for many years.

Johannes Kepler made an important contribution to this research. He was the first to state that the tides were caused by the moon. Many other scientists and mathematicians worked to further understand the movement of water in the ocean. They learned to calculate and predict the tides.

In 1799 a Frenchman named Pierre Girard and his son looked closely at ocean waves. They believed waves could power pumps and other machines. They filed the first known patent to use the energy from ocean waves. In the 1820s, brothers Wilhelm and Ernst Weber studied the motion and shapes of water waves. They became the first to test waves in lab experiments.

Growing Research

People slowly developed technology to capture ocean energy. A man named Bochaux-Praceique designed a wave energy machine around 1910. The machine powered his home in France. Beginning in the 1940s, Yoshio Masuda was a key developer of

In addition to his work on waves, Wilhelm Weber also made important contributions to the study of magnetism.

ocean wave technology. Masuda was a former officer in the Japanese navy. One of Masuda's inventions was the oscillating water column. This type of device is still used today. It harnesses the movement of waves.

Other people researched ocean temperatures. Engineer Jacques-Arsène d'Arsonval came up with the idea of ocean thermal energy conversion. D'Arsonval's student Georges Claude built the first OTEC plant in 1930. It was located in Cuba. Claude later built another plant. It was off the coast of Brazil. But conditions in the ocean destroyed both plants. Twenty years later, scientists planned to build an OTEC plant in West Africa. But the plans were too expensive to carry out. In 1974 the United States created the Natural Energy Laboratory of Hawaii Authority. This lab continues to perform OTEC research today.

In 1966 the first tidal barrage went into operation. Tidal barrages are large dams. They generate electricity from tidal power. The first barrages were

Claude's experimental power plants were unsuccessful, but his work helped pave the way for later developments.

located in France. They were at the mouth of the Rance river estuary. La Rance remained the world's largest tidal station until 2011. That year, South Korea

Telling the Future

As ocean technology has advanced, so has ocean prediction. In June 1978, the satellite Seasat began orbiting Earth. It was an important early step in gathering ocean data. Over the next decades, Seasat and other satellites sent back important information about the ocean. Scientists could study patterns in winds, wave and tidal heights, temperatures, and more. Computers have greatly improved prediction as well. The Global Ocean Observing System is the worldwide network for ocean data collection.

completed the larger Sihwa Lake Tidal Power Station.

New Option Needed

In the 1970s, it became clear that alternatives to fossil fuels were needed. World oil prices surged. Engineers, including Stephen Salter, looked for clean energy options. Salter created a device known as Salter's duck. It is also called the Edinburgh duck or the nodding duck. The device converted wave power into electricity. But by the 1980s, oil prices had dropped again. Governments

France's tidal barrage on the Rance was still in operation by 2016, 50 years after it began generating power.

stopped funding ocean energy projects. Salter's duck was not developed further.

Interest in ocean energy returned in the 1990s. It has been growing slowly ever since. Rising oil costs have played a role in this renewed interest. People also worry about the effects of fossil fuels on the

The Ocean Energy Leader

Many people think of the United Kingdom as the world leader in ocean energy. It tests more wave and tidal devices than the rest of the world combined. However, it may have competition. Many countries are trying to decrease their greenhouse gas output. Others have goals to use a certain amount of renewable energy in the future. In recent years, countries such as the United States, China, Australia, and Canada have been testing ocean energy technology.

environment. Additionally, nations are seeking ways to create their own energy supply, rather than buying energy from other countries. The European Marine Energy Centre (EMEC) was established in 2003. It is based in Orkney, Scotland. It provides scientists with sites to test tide and wave devices.

New technology brings new challenges. In his book *The Science of Ocean Waves*, J. B. Zirker discusses the challenges of wave technology:

> *So far, wave energy technology in the United States is in its infancy. . . . We have no long-term track records of the survival and maintenance costs of competing designs. We have only preliminary estimates of conversion efficiency. . . . Furthermore, the sources of funding and the overall cost of building the devices and their power lines are uncertain. That means we lack realistic estimates of the ultimate costs of electricity to consumers. So unless climate change becomes an overriding consideration, fossil fuels, with their established infrastructure, will continue to dominate the US energy market for some decades to come. Nevertheless, wave energy conversion continues to attract serious attention from the government as one more tool for transitioning to a clean energy future.*
>
> Source: J. B Zirker. The Science of Ocean Waves. Baltimore, MD: Johns Hopkins University, 2013. Print. 223.

Consider Your Audience

Adapt this passage for a different audience, such as your principal or younger friends. Write a blog post conveying this same information for the new audience. How does your post differ from the original text? Why?

OCEAN ENERGY SCIENCE AND TECHNOLOGY

Three of the most developed types of ocean energy technologies are wave, tidal, and OTEC. Wave and tidal technologies harvest energy from the water's motion. This is mechanical energy. OTEC harvests power from temperature differences in the water. This is thermal energy.

The world's first commercial wave energy device, Osprey 1, was towed into place in Scotland in 1995.

Prime Locations

Ocean energy technology is not possible in all places. The best areas for wave energy include western Scotland, northern Canada, and southern Africa. The best US locations include Hawaii, Alaska, and the West Coast. For tidal power plants, the best US locations are the Pacific Northwest and Atlantic Northeast. The highest tides in the world are found in eastern Canada and northern Scotland. Engineers also must consider the location of devices in the water. The most powerful waves are far out at sea. However, the devices must also be close enough to shore for the energy to be used on land. Engineers must find a balance between these requirements.

Wave Energy

Wave energy can be captured from surface waves. It can also be captured from pressure changes under the surface. The devices that turn waves into electricity are called wave energy converter (WEC) machines. They may be found near the shore or far offshore.

One type of WEC is a linear attenuator. This device is made of several segments. They float parallel to the waves. The segments are connected to pumps. As the waves move the segments, the pumps generate electricity. The electricity travels to shore by an underwater cable. Another type of WEC is called an overtopping device. It sits perpendicular to the waves. A steel or concrete column, known as an oscillating water column, floats upright in the water. Part of it is above the surface. An air pocket is trapped under it. Waves push air into the pocket. The air movement turns a turbine to make electricity. A third type of WEC is a point absorber. This floating device, or buoy, uses the up-and-down motion of the waves. The waves drive a generator to make electricity. The Azura device is an example of a point absorber.

Tidal Energy

Tidal energy technology creates electricity from the motion of ocean tides. Most coastal areas have two high tides and two low tides each day. When tidal waters move through a shallow, narrow area, the water moves fast enough to generate power.

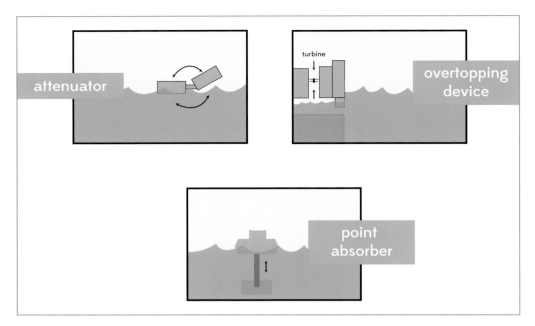

Wave Energy Devices

Types of wave energy technology include the attenuator, point absorber, and oscillating water column. What do you notice about their designs? How do the diagrams help you understand how these systems work?

There are three main types of tidal technology. The first is a barrage, or dam. In a barrage, tides are forced into an area with a turbine. The turbine spins and runs a generator that creates electricity. The second technology is a tidal turbine. A tidal turbine is similar to a wind turbine. But it is located underwater. Another technology is a tidal fence. In this system, part of the tidal flow is separated by a fence. Tidal currents spin the turbines as they pass the fence.

Ocean Thermal Energy Conversion

At the surface, ocean water is warmed by the sun. Water gets colder as it gets deeper. OTEC requires a water temperature difference of approximately 36 degrees Fahrenheit (20°C). For this reason, OTEC works best in tropical waters. An OTEC system has a pipe that brings up cold ocean water from deep below the surface. The pipe exchanges heat with the surface water to generate electricity.

Recovering Energy

The ocean holds huge amounts of energy. However, not all of this energy can be captured. The energy that actually can be used is known as recoverable energy. A 2011 study reviewed the available wave energy in the United States. It found that waves could produce 2,640 terawatt-hours of energy per year. The recoverable amount of energy is closer to 1,170 terawatt-hours per year. This would still make up one-third of the United States' yearly electricity use.

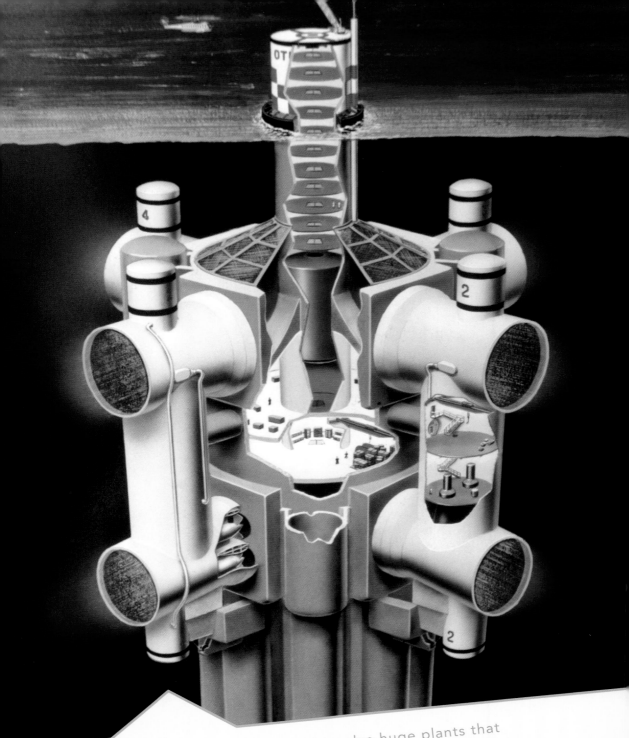

The future of OTEC could involve huge plants that generate large amounts of electricity.

There are three types of technologies used for OTEC. The first is a closed-cycle system. Warm surface water turns a fluid, such as ammonia, into a gas. The gas turns a turbine to make electricity. Then cold water turns the vapor back into liquid. The liquid gets recycled into the system. The next OTEC technology is an open-cycle system. Warm surface water is boiled to make steam. This turns a turbine to make electricity. The steam is made into freshwater. This water leaves the system. Then new water is brought in. The third OTEC technology is a hybrid system. It contains parts of the other two systems.

EXPLORE ONLINE

Chapter Three discusses different types of ocean energy. The video at the website below has more information on this topic. How is the information from the video the same as the information in Chapter Three? What new information did you learn from the website?

Ocean Energy Video
mycorelibrary.com/ocean-energy

CHAPTER FOUR

OCEAN ENERGY OUTLOOK

O cean energy has many possibilities for growth. Projects are currently underway around the world. The EMEC in the United Kingdom is the world's largest site for testing offshore ocean energy technology. Canada's Atlantic Coast has been the site of tidal energy testing. Other places, such as South Africa and Portugal, have promising

Researchers are testing new ocean energy devices in many places, including off the coast of Denmark.

The US Navy has shown interest in wave energy technology, including a device known as an energy harvesting microbuoy.

ocean energy resources too. Unfortunately, many of these areas lack funding and research opportunities.

The US Department of Energy's Water Power Program funds a number of ocean energy programs. Some develop new technology for turbines and structures. Others are trying to improve ocean predictions. The Water Power Program also sends US scientists to learn at European test sites.

Several US companies are dedicated to ocean energy. The Ocean Renewable Power Company in Maine is one of the largest today. Verdant Power leads the Roosevelt Island Tidal Energy (RITE) Project. The RITE project has several tidal turbines in New York's East River. Other companies are designing buoys and devices for wave farms. A wave farm is a group of wave devices that make electricity.

Studying the Deep

Underwater devices help scientists study the ocean remotely. These devices can gather large amounts of data in short amounts of time. They can also explore dangerous or difficult-to-reach places. They can take measurements, collect samples, record video, and more. A remotely operated vehicle (ROV) is attached to a ship by a cable. Scientists control the ROV from the ship. An autonomous underwater vehicle (AUV) does not need human control.

New Possibilities

A recent ocean technology is the tidal lagoon. A tidal lagoon uses a wall to harness tidal power. The wall extends in a big loop from the shore. Turbines in the wall generate electricity. The world's first tidal lagoon power plant is planned for Wales, in the United Kingdom. It should be completed by 2019.

Jobs in ocean energy are expected to increase in the future. Engineers will be needed to design and build devices. Oceanographers, marine ecologists, and computer experts also will be needed. Divers and other workers will be needed to help install and maintain equipment.

Making Improvements

Researchers are working to address concerns about ocean energy. The US Department of Energy is studying the environmental effects of ocean energy. Oregon State University scientists are measuring the noise of wave energy devices. Other scientists are using sonar and underwater cameras. They are

Small-scale laboratory tests can help researchers determine the efficiency of a design and predict its effect on the environment.

Northwest National Marine Renewable Energy Center

The Northwest National Marine Renewable Energy Center was created in 2008 by the US Department of Energy. It is a partnership between the University of Washington, Oregon State University, and the University of Alaska Fairbanks. This group researches and develops ocean energy. It also runs the Pacific Marine Energy Center (PMEC) off the coast of Oregon. The center includes ocean energy test sites. The group hopes people around the world will use the PMEC sites for ocean energy research and testing.

monitoring effects on fish and marine mammals. These environmental questions are some of the biggest hurdles ocean energy faces today.

There is a lot of work ahead to make ocean energy a reality. Devices need research, design, and testing. Only then will they be ready for widespread use. Engineers need to plan carefully for ocean energy locations. They must ensure devices do not disrupt views, fishing, or other activities. Another challenge is the high starting cost of

Experimental ocean energy devices show ocean energy researchers which devices work best in which areas.

ocean energy projects. In recent years, some exciting projects have been called off. This is often because of funding problems. However, supporters point out that ocean energy can pay for itself over time.

The Energy of Tomorrow?

Ocean energy technology remains in the very early stages of development. Humans have studied the ocean for centuries. But they are just beginning to learn how to harness, store, and use its power. The world's demand for energy continues to grow. People will likely turn to the ocean and other renewable energy sources. These sources offer clean alternatives to fossil fuels. Scientists and engineers will continue to study the ocean's power. The ocean could be an important and reliable energy source in the years to come.

It can be difficult for renewable energy to compete with fossil fuels. In his book *Renewable*, science writer Jeremy Shere discusses the importance of renewables in the future:

> *While it's true that vast amounts of oil, coal, and natural gas remain in the ground, it's also true that the more we discover, the more we use. . . . Eventually, whether a few decades or a few centuries from now, fossil fuels will be scarce, and we will have no choice but to rely on renewable sources of energy. How that adjustment will go . . . will depend on choices we begin making today.*

Source: Jeremy Shere. Renewable: The World-Changing Power of Alternative Energy. New York: St. Martin's Press, 2013. Print. 277.

Point of View

Shere has a favorable view of renewable energy. Why does he believe people should focus on developing renewable energy? Read back through the chapter. Do you agree? Why or why not? Does ocean energy seem like a good option?

FAST FACTS

- The ocean covers 71 percent of Earth. It makes life on Earth possible.
- Ocean energy is a type of renewable energy. Unlike the energy generated by burning fossil fuels, it will not run out.
- Ocean energy is in the early stages of development.
- Challenges of ocean energy include cost, development, location, and environmental effects.
- The three most developed types of ocean energy are wave, tidal, and ocean thermal energy conversion (OTEC).
- Wave and tidal technologies harness the motion of the ocean's water to produce electricity.
- Ocean thermal energy conversion uses the difference in water temperature to produce electricity.
- Not all ocean energy can be captured and used.

- The United Kingdom is a world leader in ocean energy.
  Work is also being done in Asia, other parts of Europe,
  and North America.
- Ocean energy has many possibilities for future growth.
  Recent projects include tidal lagoons.

STOP AND THINK

Dig Deeper

After reading this book, what questions do you still have about ocean thermal energy conversion? What about wave or tidal energy? With an adult's help, find a few reliable sources that can help you answer your questions. Then write a paragraph about what you learned.

You Are There

This book discusses early ocean energy research. Imagine you are assisting Johannes Kepler in the early 1600s. Write a letter to your friends about your studies of the ocean tides. Why is this work important? What questions do you still have about how the ocean works?

Take a Stand

Some people believe ocean energy will be an important energy source in the future. But others think there are too many disadvantages. List some of the benefits of ocean energy. Then list the disadvantages. Read through your lists. Do you think ocean energy is worth exploring? Why or why not?

Say What?

Studying ocean energy can mean learning new vocabulary. Find five words in this book you are unfamiliar with. Use a dictionary to find out what they mean. Then write the meanings in your own words. Try using each word in a sentence.

GLOSSARY

ecologists
scientists who study relationships between creatures and their environments

estuary
the area where a river flows into the sea

greenhouse gases
gases, such as carbon dioxide, that trap heat in the atmosphere

oceanographers
scientists who study the ocean

oscillating
moving back and forth

parallel
existing side by side and not intersecting

patent
the legal right to an invention

perpendicular
meeting at a 90 degree angle, in the shape of a T

sonar
a system that uses sound to locate underwater objects

thermal
energy from heat

turbine
a machine that spins to generate electricity

LEARN MORE

Books

MacQuitty, Miranda. *Eyewitness Ocean*. New York: DK Publishing, 2014.

Peppas, Lynn. *Ocean, Tidal, and Wave Energy*. New York: Crabtree, 2009.

Ward, Sarah E. *Electricity in the Real World*. Minneapolis, MN: Abdo Publishing, 2013.

Websites

To learn more about Alternative Energy, visit **booklinks.abdopublishing.com**. These links are routinely monitored and updated to provide the most current information available.

Visit **mycorelibrary.com** for free additional tools for teachers and students.

INDEX

ABOUT THE AUTHOR

Laura K. Murray is the author of more than 30 nonfiction books for children. She lives in Minnesota, far from the ocean but near plenty of lakes.